MORNING CALM

by Michael Minassian

Acknowledgements

Many of these poems (sometimes in different
form) have previously appeared in the following
periodicals, to whose editors grateful
acknowledgement is made:

Bridging Continents
Failed Haiku
Fourth & Sycamore
Haiku Highlights
Haiku Page
Haiku Universe
Janus-Scth
Modern Haiku
New Ulster
Solares Hill
Stillwater Review
THAT Literary Review
Trouvaille Review
Wales Haiku Journal

In addition, some of the poems in Section I
originally appeared in a pop-up chapbook entitled
Chuncheon Journal (2019) produced by Mojave
River Press.

I also want to thank the following small press editors who have published my work including (but not limited to) Michael Dwanye Smith, Michael Rehling, Gopal Lahiri, and Paul Chambers. Two editors (no longer with us) who helped me early in my writing career were William J. Higginson and Quentin R. Howard.

I want to extend my gratitude to the people of South Korea (and especially the members of the Buddhist community) for extending a warm and welcoming spirit on my visits there and providing inspiration for this project.

In Memorium: Firestone Feinberg (1951-2020)

Dedicated to Sue Minassian (Lee Joo Young) and my extended family in South Korea.

Special thank you also to Liana Minassian, Michael Newell, Alan Walowitz, and Robert Wexelblatt.

Front Cover Photo and Section Photos: Michael Minassian

Back Cover Photo: Sue Minassian

Book Design/Layout: Michael Minassian

Copyright 2020 Michael Minassian

Other books by Michael Minassian:

Time is Not a River 2020 (poetry)

Chapbooks:

Jack Pays a Visit, 2020. (poetry)

Chuncheon Journal, 2019 (poetry)

Around the Bend, 2017 (photography)

The Arboriculturist, 2010 (poetry)

Table of Contents

Part I – To Chuncheon and Beyond

Part II – The Way East

Part I – To Chuncheon and Beyond

BIRDS STAND

Every morning, white
feathered birds
along the lake
stand on one leg,
like an open
parenthesis waiting
for the end
of the sentence.

MORNING MIST

Tendrils of mist
from mountain peaks
touching clouds
before my eyes open.
Steam from tea
forms words
I put to paper
then give to the wind—

an offering:
both apology
and poem.

RAINY DAY

From high above
on the apartment balcony,
I watch the street below

the sidewalk crowded
with umbrellas—
wet mushrooms on two legs
        chased by rain.

SITTING

Wary of distractions,
I sit with eyes half closed

pushing the past and future aside—
it's not a case of amnesia

but my mind seems to need
something to do—

Later, I can remember
a few moments of quiet

the clock on the wall tells me
how much time has passed—

outside, the rain pauses,
clouds press in on all sides.

RAIN SLICKED STREETS

Rain slicked streets—
a darkened sky

traffic lights
and neon signs
reflected
on wet pavement—

a small boy steps
into a pool of light

overhead only
black clouds.

THROUGH THE WINDOW

Through the window
I see wind pushing
clouds above, trees below.

Dipping my finger
in my tea cup,
I move the sky alone.

TURTLES

The turtles in the lake
are so shy

even a drop of rain
chases them away.

WAKING EARLY

View of the market
across the street:

red chili peppers
drying on the rooftop

crows land
in the parking lot—

empty spaces
cloudless sky.

WRITING POETRY

Carrying notebook and pen,
I stop to rest on a park bench

writing poems under the trees—
random pine cones lie scattered
beneath the branches

like derelict memories
in a wilderness of words.

THE WELL-WORN KIMONO

Pulling a loose thread,
the kimono unravels—

somewhere in here
is a life lesson—
but for now, I cover
my nakedness
with paper and pen.

LONG GOODBYES

September rain
heavy in the afternoon –

leaves hang on
their branches—

long goodbyes
as autumn pauses.

A SIMPLE ACT

Sitting across from a friend
drinking afternoon tea,
watching her peel an apple—
the scent of the fruit
rising like the mist
from a mountain stream.

Reminding me of long lunches
at my grandparent's house—
their hands with skin like rice paper

wielding a sharp knife
cutting away the red road
to the apple's crisp and fragrant flesh
in one long continuous loop.

A simple act—
what is memory
but an outer membrane
covering a fruitful life,
the taste of snow,
the crunch of time.

THE FAMILY SHRINE

Squeezing through the locked gate,
I climb cracked stone steps
on the hilltop
to the deserted family shrine—

a half open door beckons and I enter,
expecting to see a statue or incense
and candles on the altar—

but there is nothing,
only dust and quiet—
behind a half open curtain
I see a painting of a standing woman

staring out at me, eyes as clear
as the cool autumn air
from long years past—

then I hear music
and a faint chanting
just outside the window

and wonder
if it is my imagination,
or the wind,
or the woman's
whispered song.

THE WATERFALL

Just off the mountain path,
I stop to rest at a pond;

A waterfall sprays mist—

like liquid, words spill
from my tongue.

AUTUMN

When I started
up the mountain path
the sun warmed my back—

later, as I walked down,
the cool shade
reminded me
summer was over.

CHEONGPYEONG-SA

On Obong-san Mountain
Cheongpyeong-sa temple
sits in lotus.

In front of the thousand
year old altar,
I bow to the Buddha

The Buddha wakes the mountain.
The mountain lifts the Buddha—
I bow again.

THROWING COINS

On the temple grounds
next to a stone bridge,
I saw a small pond
and a statue
of the Buddha
standing in a small
cut-out of rock

visitors throwing
coins in the pond,
and at the foot
of the statue

their wishes rippling
on the waters
long after they
are gone.

THE CUCKOO'S SONG

On the mountain trail
high above Chuncheon,
near the ancient temple,
I hear the call of the cuckoo—

My wife says it is good luck
to hear the cuckoo's song,
so I put the sound
in my pocket
saving it for later.

AT NIGHT

This mountain path to the temple
crowded with visitors and monks.

In the distance, clouds
hover over the mountain—
the wind holds its breath.

At night nothing remains
but the wind—
the rest will come again.

TEMPLE BELLS

At the temple, the monks asleep—
lanterns sway in the wind;

temple bells chime
filling gaps in dreams.

MOUNTAIN TEMPLE

The mountain temple
over 1200 years old—

at night,
that same moon.

AT THE FISH MARKET

after Basho

In the fish market,
black eyes frozen—
white ice crystals blink.

THE GRAVES OF KINGS

     In Gyeongju,
ancient burial mounds:
ring the city—

the writing on the stones
long ago worn by rain
and snow and wind;

the mounds covered
with tall grasses

amid bamboo shoots
mixed with wildflowers
the color of forgetfulness.

신 흥 사
Sinheungsa 新興寺
울 산 바 위
흔 들 바 위
Heundeulbawi Rock
금 강 굴
Geumganggul
비 선 대
Biseondae
커피볶는한옥
Coffee Roasting

Part II–The Way East: Selected Haiku & Senryu.

1.

This foggy morning
clouds on the sidewalk
breath of rain.

2.

Watching black clouds
for some sign of rain,
I stare at puddles on the road.

3.

Rain all night
flooded streets
sky the color of mud.

4.

Sensing rain
frogs wake me at dawn –
early morning mist.

5.

Rain splatters
against the window –
tears bend, flowers break.

6.

After last night's rain
the air smells
like the bottom of the sky.

7.

Morning thunder rumbles—
the sound approaching
like two clouds clapping.

8.

Afternoon storms arrive –
clouds so thick
they slice like bread.

9.

Mountain on the horizon –
cumulous clouds
sunlit summit mirage.

10.

Dawn breaks behind clouds –
pond reflects
rain streaked sky.

11.

Bright sunlight –
speckled clouds.
Shadows above, below.

12.

Gray clouds block
out the sun
the wind still comes.

13.

Clouds piled up
the sun waiting
for the wind.

14.

This morning's sky
no room for clouds
only blue and more blue.

15.

Crisp blue sky
cool autumn wind
did anyone tell the sun?

16.

Cold winter morning
no wind
to push the clouds.

17.

First day of the year
cold wind clears clouds—
ice rims the sun.

18.

I cannot name the wind
that has no mind
only wind.

19.

The wind speaks
through the trees—
whispers in the grass.

20.

Cold January morning
even when there is no wind
there is wind.

21.

Clouds overhead
the wind quiet—
no bell sound.

22.

Cold winter wind—
beneath the clouds
more wind.

23.

Cool edge of autumn
grey skies press—
wind ahead of itself.

24.

Silent boulders
on the mountaintop—
the wind howls still.

25.

Painting the wind
the brush finds
empty space.

26.

Dark clouds gathering
birds grow quiet—
I hold my breath.

27.

From branch to branch
a flash of red—
bird song.

28.

Cloudless blue sky
washed by rain and wind—
still room for the black crow.

29.

Arms folded,
watching birds
take flight.

30.

A sleeping bird—
under its wing
the sound of the wind.

31.

Tonight's full moon
floods the sky—
disappearing stars.

32.

First day of winter
summer thorns
sharp as love's burn.

33.

Tree branches bare—
no leaves left
to block the sun

34.

The undergrowth
along the path—
scent of hidden words.

35.

Stirring the tea
honey the first taste
on the tip of the tongue.

36.

Last night's moon
clouds come and go—
the sky blinks.

37.

Three o'clock in the morning
sleep turns on and off
like a broken toy.

38.

Tai Chi class—
instructor changes position
we bump into each other.

39.

The full moon reflected
in my wine glass
drunk with light.

40.

This haiku needs ink & brush
some calligraphy
to make a poem with one stroke.

41.

Putting out the kitchen fire
I throw a haiku
into the flames, then one more.

42.

On a chain link fence,
yesterday's newspaper
flattened by the wind.

43.

In a bowl of water
bees swim,
flower petals float.

44.

Yellow tulips
in the back yard—
last week's rain.

45.

Her scent lingers
on the letter –
delicate spice winged words.

46.

First touch of morning
across the bed—
life's long thread.

47.

Trees hold memories
of sailing ships—
each leaf a drowned sailor.

48.

The wind pushes leaves
from tree to ground –
a rustling skirt.

49.

Darkness deceives
as morning arrives,
blinking its eye the sun.

50.

Yes, she said,
the answer
is still no.

51.

This cold winter night
your house dark –
tire tracks in the snow.

52.

Tonight's full moon
floods the sky
blotting out the stars.

53.

Dogwood blooming
all along the path
the trees' bark all I hear.

54.

Black sand beach
volcanic rock—
water cools fire.

55.

Train whistle blows
fading soundtrack—
sleepless nights.

56.

Falling off a cliff,
I discovered I could fly –
soft landing, hard lesson.

57.

A red and brown leaf
pasted on the page –
notebook from the past.

58.

Clouds breaking up this morning—
time for one short poem
before the sun appears.

59.

That cloud shaped like an ear—
if I shout, I'm sure
it would hear me

60.

The cold winter air
blew away my last thought
- ah, growing old.

38선
THE 38TH PARALLEL
38선

Part III – The Way Back

THE 38TH PARALLEL

The border shifted long ago
the lake clear and clean

watching clouds
bump into hills

I imagine soldiers
lying buried in the earth

bones bleached white
beneath green grasses

this space now quiet
sky and waters a calm blue

only herons restless
on the bank.

EARLY MORNING MIST

Morning mist rises
from the mountains—

the sun brushes
the sky in one stroke—

yellow paint, blue dye.

RIPPLES

A bird flutters
in the treetop;
its song falls
likes rain:

ripples
        ripples
                in the sky.

A DROP OF MEMORY

Down the path
in a clearing just
past a grove of trees

I sat on a boulder
dropped by giants
on their way home

a gray drop of memory
still warm from the sun.

BOTH WINGS

The one-legged bird
that visits
my backyard,
hops across the lawn
then flies off
on both wings.

THE BLANK PAGE

I'm scraping
at these words
until my fingernails bleed

tonight I will write
them in the rain.

THE BUDDHAS KEEP WATCH

Along the grey wall
of the temple grounds,
visitors place small
Buddha statues
made of stone, wood,
and plastic

some painted,
others bare—

(a few scattered coins
remain on the wall)

having nothing to offer,
I find a red leaf still on the branch
but the tree resists—

I leave empty handed

the Buddhas' eyes follow me
as I walk down the path.

THE OLD TEMPLE

Dropped off on the mountain road,
I walk uphill for thirty minutes
to reach Weolcheon-sa
temple near the peak—

finding only a caretaker
and his wife,
water bowls dry,
candles and incense unlit.

A layer of dust
everywhere,
only Buddha statues
lined up on the altar
swept clean.

The sun slanting in
through the open door
the statues' shadows
cast against the wall—

A breeze wandering in,
trees whispering leaves,
      no bell sound.

I HAVE LEARNED
THE KOREAN ALPHABET

I have learned the alphabet:
Hangul, a phonetic system,
and practice sounding
out the words
though their meaning,
elusive as the white crane
in the northern marshes,
slips through my fingers
like the mist before
the morning rain.

I have learned the words
for polite conversation,
to say excuse me or I am sorry,
hello, thank you, and sleep well;
I know how to say
I am hungry, I am full, I am tired,
I am in love with your hair,
your skin, your eyes
every morning I taste your lips
searching for the connection
between symbol and sound
silence and flesh
drawing the letters
in the air as if language
was the fabric of touch.

I LIKE WATCHING KOREAN DRAMAS

The King appears to be surrounded
by sycophants who smile
and bow, then plot his death

while rival factions pile up dead
bodies like woodsmen felling trees,
stacking up cords of corpses
outside the palace wall.

The serving women stay bent
in a permanent pose while standing
still, and the eunuchs, mutilated

as young boys, remain unshaven,
wearing the characteristic green robes,
(symbolic of what I am not sure)
and manage to outlive
the kings several times over.

Later, when I practice my few
Korean words, my wife laughs,
then explains these are all archaic terms
.
as if I were an air traffic controller
speaking in iambic pentameter:
("My planes fly up/some flights remain below")

And she refuses to call me King
in any language, or practice archery
in the living room, although she lets me

check my food with a silver spoon—
the traditional test, she says, for poison,
laughing since I cooked the meal myself.

TO PAINT THE WORLD

I hear you in the next room
talking on your phone;

the low murmur of your voice
lulls me into a half-sleep

like an old box of letters:
cancelled stamps and footprints

in the dust. When you laugh, I am
jolted awake. Now the conversation

seems to be one-sided. I hear you
mmmm, and then say goodbye

in Korean, a language you patiently
taught me to recognize, all twenty-four

characters and their multiple
combinations, piled so high

I slept under them like a child
waiting outside the teacher's home

high up in the mountains
where birds carried tubes of words

in their claws, squeezing color
to paint the world, to speak in song.

UNDER THE KIMONO

My love keeps watch
as I change my clothes –
stripped down to
a bare notion of time,
I can sense the skeleton
of her thoughts.

She recites long Korean poems
in my ear and I dream
of snow-covered trees
that line mountain passes,
and tiger tracks leading
to manacled clouds,
as mandalas of colored
sand slip through my fingers
like an illogically
early moonrise
I can stir with my finger
by the edge of a lidless lake.

BIRD'S NEST

Rebirth is a tricky concept—
even harder to remember
a previous life—

once an embryo within an egg,
waiting to hatch inside the nest—
the bird's song enough

to make me pause and wonder:
is that one of my own—
the colored feathers and beak,

the heart beating one hundred
times a minute when in flight—
slower when perched on the branch:

which call do I answer:
the first song of the morning
or the last note at moon's rise.

TEMPLESTAY

After dark, incense smoke
drifts through the temple.

Monks bow in a row—
Buddha statues silent
as we go to our rooms.

At the Zen temple
even the wind whispers
who are you?

UNDER THE MOONLIGHT

I

Too many clouds
crowd *Obong* mountain;
the rocks shaped
like soldiers along
the steep paths;
at night, I hear
voices through
the pine trees:
long lost friends.

II

I haven't had a drink
since spring began
and flowers bloomed
on the mountainside
three weeks ago –
why do I feel drunk?
why do I weep
under the moonlight?

III

When I grow tired
of gazing at the moon,
I'll watch its reflection
on the surface of the river.

Each night, the waters
flow past, high and low –
perhaps in my next life
swimming past this same spot
I'll see the moon again.

Copyright© 2020 Michael Minassian
ISBN: 978-93-88319-17-1

First Edition: 2020
Rs. 200/-

Cyberwit.net
HIG 45 Kaushambi Kunj, Kalindipuram
Allahabad - 211011 (U.P.) India
http://www.cyberwit.net
Tel: +(91) 9415091004 +(91) (532) 2552257
E-mail: info@cyberwit.net

No part of this book may be reproduced or transmitted in any form or by
any means, electronic, mechanical, photocopying, or otherwise, without
the express written consent of Michael Minassian.

Printed at Repro India Limited.

www.ingramcontent.com/pod-product-compliance
Lightning Source LLC
Chambersburg PA
CBHW050611160726
48003CB00003B/1135